Wise Owl's
ABC BOOK
A Book of Small Creatures

by Dorothy Fay Richards
illustrated by Helen Endres
created by Child's World

 CHILDRENS PRESS, CHICAGO

Library of Congress Cataloging in Publication Data

Richards, Dorothy Fay, 1915-
  Wise Owl's ABC book.

  (Wise Owl plus)
  SUMMARY: Wise Owl meets a variety of
animals on an alphabet walk.
  [1. Alphabet. 2. Animals—Fiction]
I. Endres, Helen. II. Title.
PZ7.R379Wh   [E]   81-6187
ISBN 0-516-06561-0   AACR2

"Enough! Come here. It's time for a talk. I think we should take an alphabet walk!

"We'll meet some friends along the way. The alphabet begins with A.

Aa

''A is for ANT.

Bb

"B is for BUTTERFLY.

C c

''C is for CATERPILLAR.

Dd

''D is for DRAGONFLY.

8

Ee

''E is for EAGLET.

Ff

"F is for FROG.

Gg

''G is for GRASSHOPPER.

Hh

''H is for HUMMINGBIRD.

Ii

"I is for INCHWORM.

Jj

"J is for JUNE BUG.

Kk

"K is for KATYDID.

L l

"L is for LADYBUG.

Mm

''M is for MANTIS.

Nn

''N is for NEWT.

O o

"O is for OWLET.

Pp

''P is for POLLIWOG.

Qq

"Q is for QUAIL.

Rr

''R is for RABBIT.

Ss

''S is for SQUIRREL.

Tt

''T is for TURTLE.

Uu

UNCLE
POSIE
OWL

''U is for UNCLE.

V v

"V is for VOLE.

26

Ww

"W is for WOODPECKER.

Xx

"There are no animals whose names
start with X. But the woodpecker left
his mark. X is for X!

"Y is for YELLOW Jacket. His sting isn't nice. Here he comes now. Run for your life!

Zz

''Back home at last—with one letter
left. This one's about me. Z is for ZZZZ. . . .''

A Wise Owl Plus

Now as a plus, match these letters and friends. Can you find the letter that begins each friend's name?

A B C D E F G H I J K L M N O P Q R

Z Y X W V U T S